REDRAWING *the* MAP

The Unification and Reunification of Germany

JACKIE F. STANMYRE

Cavendish Square
New York

Cataloging-in-Publication Data

Names: Stanmyre, Jackie F.
Title: The unification and reunification of Germany / Jackie F. Stanmyre.
Description: New York : Cavendish Square, 2019. | Series: Redrawing the map | Includes glossary and index.
Identifiers: ISBN 9781502635709 (pbk.) | ISBN 9781502635686 (library bound) | ISBN 9781502635693 (ebook)
Subjects: LCSH: Germany--Juvenile literature. | Berlin (Germany)--Politics and government--1945-1990--Juvenile literature. | Germany--History--Unification, 1990--Juvenile literature.
Classification: LCC DD17.K56 2019 | DDC 943--dc23
Names: Stanmyre, Jackie F.
Title: The unification and reunification of Germany / Jackie F. Stanmyre.
Description: New York : Cavendish Square, 2019. | Series: Redrawing the map | Includes glossary and index.
Identifiers: ISBN 9781502635709 (pbk.) | ISBN 9781502635686 (library bound) | ISBN 9781502635693 (ebook)
Subjects: LCSH: Germany--Juvenile literature. | Berlin (Germany)--Politics and government--1945-1990--Juvenile literature. | Germany--History--Unification, 1990--Juvenile literature.
Classification: LCC DD17.K56 2019 | DDC 943--dc23

Editorial Director: David McNamara
Editor: Erin L. McCoy
Copy Editor: Michele Suchomel-Casey
Associate Art Director: Amy Greenan
Designer: Jessica Nevins
Production Coordinator: Karol Szymczuk
Photo Research: J8 Media

CONTENTS

CHAPTER ONE

Germany's Long Journey to Unity

Maps of Germany as it is today show one united country, with a single government and a national constitution. Germany didn't always have the same borders, however; instead, they're the product of a long history of war, cultural and political clashes, influential leaders, and empire-building. Germany was born, hundreds of years ago, as a confederation of city-states that varied in their culture, traditions, and style of government. Those city-states unified on January 18, 1871, but the borders of Germany were still far from set; they have been redrawn again and again over the past 150 years.

Opposite: Modern-day Germany (*shown at center in light green*) is a united country with a single government for all its people.

Unification

The German Confederation, consisting of thirty-nine city-states, was founded by the Congress of Vienna in 1815. The states that comprised it were very different from one another. Some guaranteed certain civil rights and had constitutions, while others did not. Prussia and especially Austria were the most influential of these states. The confederation had no central authority, but as other European countries moved toward democracy, Germans would take notice. Many wanted to be a part of a single country, ruled by a single government.

The early days of unity were accomplished after the creation of the Frankfurt Parliament, which developed Germany's first national constitution in 1849. Germany later expanded its power under the leadership of Otto von Bismarck by engaging in wars, often against France. The nation's first major territorial gain was Alsace and Lorraine in 1871. This acquisition proved a major victory, as the region was a center of industrial production, notable for its valuable iron ore deposits. German exports tripled.

The success of this annexation encouraged further expansion, and in the late 1800s and early 1900s, Germany passed bills to finance the rapid construction of a world-class imperial navy. The goal was to acquire more colonies.

Germany entered into World War I as a world power. Its primary strength in the war was the use of U-boats, or submarines. Its policy was to sink any ships

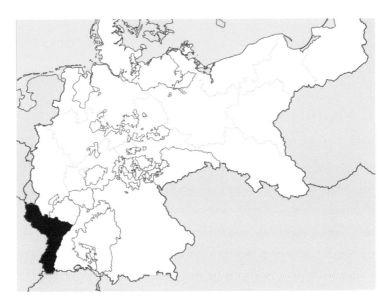

Alsace and Lorraine (*shown in red*) were significant gains for the young German nation, as they provided an extraordinary opportunity for Germany to increase its export market.

that crossed its path, which initially led to victories. The 1918 Treaties of Brest-Litovsk awarded Germany parts of Poland, the Baltic States, Finland, and Ukraine in exchange for a cessation of hostilities. However, the United States' entrance into the war in 1917 made Germany a new enemy. Less than two years after Germany expanded its hold on Europe, the Treaty of Versailles was ratified, forcing Germany to relinquish its hold on those territories it had just acquired.

After WWI ended, the Weimar Republic was established in another attempt at a unifying German government. The leadership, however, was weak, and many citizens blamed them for the Germans' loss in

WWI. This discontent opened the door for the rise of extremist parties, including the National Socialist German Workers' Party, later known as the Nazis.

Division and Reunification

Adolf Hitler's ascension within the German government coincided with grand national ambitions of expanding German territory and propagated what the Nazis called the Aryan race—light-skinned individuals whom Nazis and white supremacists believed to be superior to other people. A power-hungry Hitler ravaged Europe during World War II, conquering the Rhineland and parts of Czechoslovakia. He then partnered with the Soviet Union—normally a German enemy—and its leader, Joseph Stalin, to take over Poland. From there, Hitler's military moved through Denmark, Norway, Belgium, the Netherlands, and Luxembourg. The Americans were aiding Great Britain, which made an invasion too challenging. Hitler broke the German-Soviet Nonaggression Pact he had signed with the Soviet Union and moved to conquer its capital of Moscow. This was the beginning of the end of German conquest, as a cold Russian winter and strengthened Allied armies led to German defeats in the east, then the west.

The Germans were on the losing side of World War II. At the Potsdam Conference in 1945, Germany was divided into four occupation zones controlled by the United States, Britain, and France—all members of the Allied powers—and the Soviet Union. The Allies

A DIVIDED COUNTRY

Germany may be unified now, but most of its citizens, after World War II, never thought they'd return to being one country.

joined their zones together to create a single democratic government, which came to be known as the Federal Republic of Germany. The Soviets developed the German Democratic Republic in the east, and it was run as a satellite Communist state.

Perhaps these neighboring states could have lived peacefully, despite their extremely different ideologies, were it not for the location of Germany's capital. Berlin was entirely surrounded by the Soviet part of German territory, but the Allied powers had control over the western part of the city. This arrangement would prove to be troublesome. The Berlin Wall was built in 1961, physically dividing the city.

East Germans under Soviet rule didn't have the same economic opportunities that their western counterparts did, and many made attempts to flee the country. The Cold War diminished the strength of Communism and the Soviets, which ultimately led to the dismantling of the wall in 1989.

After forty-five years of division, the two German countries reunited officially in 1990. Most citizens considered this a favorable outcome, but the changes forced upon Germans in both the east and west as a result of reunification have been tumultuous and difficult in the decades since.

GERMAN CONFEDERATION, 1815–1866

CHAPTER TWO

Unification and the Impact of World War I

The stage was first set for German unification in 1813, following the Battle of Leipzig, when a coalition of the Russian, Prussian, Austrian, and Swedish armies defeated Napoleon Bonaparte and the French. The German states, as members of the Confederation of the Rhine, originally had sided with French emperor Napoleon but defected to join the coalition when his defeat seemed imminent. With this, Prussia again became one of Europe's great powers.

The Congress of Vienna was convened from November 1814 to June 1815 to restore order to a European continent that had been largely controlled by the rise and fall in power of Napoleon. The convention was attended by delegates from Europe's great powers, including Austria, Prussia, Britain, Russia, and France, as well as more than two hundred representatives from

Opposite: The German Confederation, shown at left as it was between 1815 and 1866, was first formed as a group of city-states. Prussia and Austria were the largest powers.

separate states, cities, religious orders, and associations. The goals of the congress were well understood: to redraw Europe's territorial borders, settle political disputes, and deal with the destabilized central European government following the fall of the Holy Roman Empire.

Of all those in attendance, Germany was perhaps most affected by the outcome. The Final Act of Vienna established the German Confederation, made up of thirty-nine sovereign states and four free cities. The states, however, were only loosely aligned with each other, and the idea of a single German identity— and single German state—was still many decades in the future.

The German Confederation

Among the important territories to become a part of the German Confederation was the Ruhr, an industrial hotbed with access to three major rivers. By the 1850s, the Ruhr valley was home to three hundred coal mines fueling blast furnaces that turned iron ore into steel. This steel was often used in the manufacturing of machines, steam engines, and armaments or weaponry.

Meanwhile, the ideas of the Enlightenment era were starting to gain traction in Germany. The Enlightenment was a movement throughout Europe during the eighteenth century that focused on expanding intellectual and philosophical ideals such as liberty, tolerance, constitutional government, and a separation of church and state. The leadership of the German Confederation did not appear to support these principles. However, leaders within the individual German states started pushing for these reforms. Some changes included the protection of free speech rights, the formation of individual constitutional governments, and the establishment of laissez-faire economic policies that created a free market, without governmental interference into the economy.

German states were most successful in their ambitions related to freeing up trade opportunities within the confederation. They promoted this goal by adopting a common currency and addressing river and road tolls and customs duties that had once made trade within the country expensive. The German customs union, Zollverein, originally established by the Prussians, greatly expanded between 1834—when it was founded—and 1860. It came to include most of the German Confederation states, including larger constituents such as Baden, Bavaria, Saxony, Thuringia, and Württemberg.

Attempts at Unity

The result of the German customs union was more far-reaching than just allowing the German states to trade goods. It also stimulated the German economy and promoted industrialization, including steel and coal production. Railway systems greatly expanded, and as the economy grew, so did the middle class. This would change the face of the country because the middle class was full of people with liberal ideas who were also growing more enthusiastic about their German identity, including the shared culture, language, and history of the German people. However, Austria's foreign minister, Klemens, Fürst von Metternich, was a key proponent of the conservative status quo and opposed the idea of German unity, arguing that the Austrian Empire, multicultural as it was, would not fit neatly into a united German state.

The liberal and conservative masses met in discord during the March Revolution of 1848. The lower classes' opportunities had been decimated by industrialization, and they turned to the writings of Karl Marx and Friedrich Engels, in particular *The Communist Manifesto* (1848), which advocated socialism and the rise to power of the working classes. But the middle classes, called the bourgeoisie in Marxist terminology, responded ardently: they demonstrated in the streets of Berlin, demanding that Prussian king Frederick William IV grant them a constitution, a representative parliament, and freedom of speech. The king was forced to agree.

The result was the new national assembly, known as the Frankfurt Parliament, which first convened on May 18, 1848. After much debate, particularly over whether or not to include Austria in its new nation, the parliament ratified a constitution on March 28, 1849. But the vote had barely passed, and the constitution was not recognized by many of the confederation's major states. A unified Germany was still more a vision than a reality.

The Frankfurt Parliament established a constitutional monarchy and offered the crown to Frederick William IV. He refused to accept it, which spurred a conservative backlash. By June 1849, the parliament had crumbled to nothing. The revolution's leaders were mostly dead, imprisoned, or in exile.

Austria and Prussia: Battling for Dominance

Conservative governance was in place for the next decade until the rise of Prussian statesman Otto von Bismarck. He believed the Prussian state could only compete with other European powers as the head of a unified German nation-state that excluded Austria. Given the previous failure at unity, Bismarck believed that war would be the only route to a unified Germany. In an impassioned 1862 speech that would become famous, Bismarck said: "It is not by speeches and majority resolutions that the great questions of the time are decided—that was the big mistake of 1848 and 1849—but by iron and blood." The Prussian parliament refused Bismarck's demands to increase funding for military expenditures, but he ignored them and raised the funds for a war anyway.

Frederick William IV ultimately forced the Prussians to rejoin the German Confederation. However, although tensions were high, Prussia and Austria would join together a last time during the wars of Schleswig-Holstein, which helped to expand German

Otto von Bismarck was an early visionary for German unity. He believed Austria should be excluded from the German nation.

territory and would also involve citizens of German descent. Prussia, with the help of Austria, defeated the Danish army during these conflicts. As a result, Prussia acquired the region of Schleswig, while Austria acquired Holstein. These regions included productive Baltic Sea ports, useful in growing Germany's power.

The Second Schleswig War made obvious Prussia's military might, which it would soon put to use again. The Prussian army was outnumbered in the Austro-Prussian War of 1866, but it was equipped with new industrial technologies and modern warfare. The Prussians triumphed, and in place of the now-dissolved German Confederation, Prussia formed the North German Federation, including all twenty-one German states north of the Main River. Prussia also annexed Schleswig-Holstein and former Austrian allies Hanover, Nassau, and Hesse-Kassel. The North German Federation was under the control of the Hohenzollern dynasty and encompassed all of north Germany.

War and Unity

Bismarck, meanwhile, was seeking full unity. He determined that, if southern and northern Germans had a common enemy, their chances of uniting once and for all would be greatly improved—so Bismarck set his sights on France.

At the same time, Spain was attempting to fill its vacant throne and was eyeing Prince Leopold, a relative of the Prussian monarch. The French hated the idea of a Prussian-Spanish alliance and threatened to take arms

The territory of Schleswig-Holstein (*shown in red*) was desirable because of its access to ports on the Baltic Sea.

against Prussia unless Prince Leopold refused to accept the crown. This conflict gave Bismarck an opening.

Bismarck took the correspondence—called the Ems telegram—between the French ambassador and King William I of Prussia, brother of Frederick William IV, and altered it to make it seem as though the two men had insulted each other. On July 13, 1870, Bismarck sent this edited version to foreign diplomats and the press in order to increase tensions between France and Prussia. It worked. The French declared war on Prussia on July 19, 1870, convincing Prussians and Germans from all reaches of the North German Federation that France was the aggressor.

Prussia, the North German Confederation, and the south German states banded together to prepare for war against the French. They converged quickly on the battlefield, while the less-prepared French worked to get their military together. The French military would not be fast enough or large enough. Less than six months after war was declared, the French were forced to surrender their capital city of Paris on January 19, 1871. The day before, however, was the monumental moment in Germany's quest for unity: Hohenzollern leader William I was crowned emperor of the united German Empire.

Bismarck, who was named chancellor, continued acting in the Prussian interest. The government was set up to include delegates from other German states, but Prussia held veto power—the ability to overrule the opinions of all the other states.

Territorial Expansion and Social Change

A few months after the Germans declared victory over France, the unified country laid claim to even more territory. On May 10, 1871, the Treaty of Frankfurt ceded the territories of Alsace and Lorraine to Germany. These would prove important as Germany continued its quest to become a global power.

Alsace and Lorraine contributed to Germany's ability to become a leader in industrial production due to the presence of iron ore deposits there. Power and influence on an international scale was largely attained by those countries with robust coal and steel production. German exports tripled, and the newly formed nation became the European leader in exports—second in the world behind only the United States.

But Germany wanted more. In order to grow its power, the country first focused its efforts on the development of a world-class navy. The reason for this focus was twofold: Germany wanted to protect its access to sea-based trade, and it wanted a means to expand its empire—that is, to find and acquire future German colonies. Between 1898 and 1912, a series of bills were passed to increase naval spending. Grand Admiral Alfred von Tirpitz focused on building massive battleships.

The British, who had the world's largest fleet of ships, were worried about Germany's fast growth and

The crew of the German first battleship division leaves for China on July 11, 1900. In the late 1800s and early 1900s, German leadership emphasized the establishment of a large German navy. They intended to continue expanding German borders.

were seeking allies. In April 1904, the British and French governments ended almost a century of feuding by signing the Entente Cordiale. The German desire for more power grew as it realized that its enemies were setting aside their differences.

Germany wanted to test this new relationship between the British and French. Germany's leader at the time, William II, stated his support for Moroccan independence during a state visit to Tangiers. The French, however, considered the Moroccan region to be under their influence. Would the British come to the French's defense? The short answer was yes. German chancellor Bernhard, prince von Bülow, proposed a meeting of countries to resolve the issue of Morocco. The French were upset and reluctant to attend, but the British ultimately convinced them that it was in their best interest to address the matter peacefully. At the Algeciras Conference, France was granted control over Morocco. However, and perhaps even more importantly, Germany gained a greater understanding of where it stood in the international playing field: at the conference, Austria-Hungary had supported Germany, while Great Britain, Italy, Russia, Spain, and the United States had all backed France.

The following year, the British and Russians came together at the Anglo-Russia Convention. Long rivals, the British and Russians agreed to support each other militarily against Germany. The three great imperial world powers—Great Britain, France, and Russia—had all reached formal agreements about how to function alongside and support each other. Germany was the outsider.

Within its own boundaries, the German story was different. The united country was flourishing. Its economy continued to expand dramatically. The steel output of Germany was more than double that of Great Britain. The German population grew by 40 percent between 1890 and 1913—although, despite the country's economic success, living standards for many were poor.

Women, as a group, saw dramatic change in their status as citizens around the turn of the twentieth century. More middle-class women were working than ever before. As they began to play a growing role in the economy, they took the opportunity to voice their desire for more political rights. In 1894, the Bund Deutscher Frauenvereine (Federation of German Women's Associations) was formed to fight for women's political and workplace rights. By 1908, women could formally join political parties, and in 1918, they won the right to vote.

Meanwhile, nationalism was at its peak. Leading intellectuals were pushing forward the German cause, voicing grand ambition for the united state. One such voice was that of Heinrich von Treitschke, a professor at Humboldt University of Berlin. He thought the German destiny was to acquire a colonial empire, challenge Great Britain's power, and suppress socialism. "No nation has greater cause than we to hold in honour the memory of our hard-struggling fathers, or recalls so seldom how through their blood and tears, their sweat of brain and of hand, the blessing of its unity has been won," he wrote. Treitschke's passion for German nationalism spurred similar sentiments among the people.

The idea of German unity had long been about a common people sharing a country. The subtext of this message was that those who were different didn't belong. In the beginning, this mostly meant the Austrians. But Treitschke, in writing about German history, said that the Jewish people were a threat to national unity because they didn't fully embrace the ideal of cultural assimilation. A person who is culturally assimilated would be said to have adopted the same values and ways of life as those in the majority culture. In point of fact, most German Jews were very assimilated to German culture and largely supportive of German unity. Nonetheless, Treitschke and others argued that if Jews were to stay in Germany, it might mean a threat to German unity—an idea that would gain strength over the decades to come.

World War I

Tensions were brewing elsewhere in Europe. The events that led up to World War I began in the Balkans, where a range of people of varying descents were interested in moving toward independence as nation-states. Two Balkan wars were fought in the early eighteenth century to determine who would rule the territories and how

Women from around the world attend the 25th congress of the International Alliance of Women's Suffrage and Equal Citizenship, which took place in Berlin in June 1929.

they would be partitioned. Passions were running high, and several groups were unhappy with the outcomes, particularly the Bosnians.

One Bosnian in particular finally sparked the war that had already been brewing in Europe for years. Gavrilo Princip, a South Slav nationalist, was fuming over the Austrian annexation of Bosnia-Herzegovina. He assassinated Archduke Franz Ferdinand and his wife, Sophie Chotek Ferdinand. Franz Ferdinand had been next in line for the Austro-Hungarian throne.

The dynamics of Europe were entangled at the time. This conflict could not exist exclusively between these two countries because of all of the alliances and relationships each had with other nations throughout

Europe. After the assassination, European countries had to take sides. Russia supported the Serbians, who were also of Slavic descent; France, per the Franco-Russian alliance, was willing to support Russia in the case of military involvement. Turkey, however, signed an alliance with Germany, which had set itself up to fight a war on two fronts: against Russia to the east and France to the west—a surprisingly bold commitment, considering that Germany had little involvement in the initial conflict.

The German people nonetheless supported the war fervently. They wanted a chance to show off their strength and were sure they would win—especially since the Germans already had a plan in place. Developed in the early 1890s, the Schlieffen Plan was designed to guide Germany should it ever face a two-front war. According to the plan, France should be defeated first; it even mapped an invasion through the neutral territories of Luxembourg and Belgium. The belief was that Austria would begin by targeting Russia, and Germany would join Austria in this effort after securing France.

However, two unforeseen factors would soon dampen the success of the Germans: first, Italy claimed

THE UNITED STATES' ROLE IN WORLD WAR I

If the United States had never entered World War I, Germany may have held onto those territories that it later ended up losing.

A German crew evacuates and surrenders their U-boat in the North Atlantic in November 1917. German U-boats were one of the military's main strategic forces during World War I.

neutrality, ignoring the promises of the Triple Alliance signed in 1882 by Austria, Germany, and Italy. This left the German and Austrian forces with no other outside support. Second, Belgium was supposed to have been neutral ground, according to a treaty signed in 1837. As soon as Germany used Belgium as part of its route to France, the United Kingdom joined the war, protesting Germany's violation of that neutrality. The Germans had no more allies, and they had even more enemies.

The reasons for the downfall of Germany were multifold and complicated, as it fought against opponents on several fronts. However, a major turning point in the war came with the United States' entrance and its formal alliance with the Allied powers. Despite the fact that the United States had cultural and economic ties to Great Britain, the country had intended to remain neutral and uninvolved in the European affair.

The United States did, however, provide munitions and financial assistance to the Allies. Germany took this to mean that the United States' statement of "neutrality" could not be trusted. When the German naval force was tested in a seemingly do-or-die onslaught, it disregarded the idea of keeping away from the Americans.

The Germans' use of U-boats was imperative in fighting against the strong British navy. However, its tactics with those submarines led to its final downfall. The Germans engaged in what was termed "unrestricted submarine warfare," meaning that anyone could be a potential target. In 1916, following the sinking of an unarmed French boat called the *Sussex*, United States president Woodrow Wilson threatened to sever diplomatic relations with Germany. He insisted that Germany stop its unrestricted submarine warfare by sparing passenger ships and by allowing the crews of enemy ships to abandon their vessels prior to attack. Germany accepted those terms in what came to be known as the Sussex Pledge.

However, by January 1917, the desperate Germans saw their underwater fighting tactics as the quickest way to beat the British, and they ignored their pledge. The Germans believed that, even if the United States were incensed enough by this to dispatch military forces, the Germans would have long since defeated the British before US boats could land in Europe. Germany reengaged in unrestricted submarine warfare.

In the meantime, Germany had also pledged to the Mexican government that it would help the Mexicans gain back territory lost in the Mexican-American War in return for their support. United States officials received word of this news through the Zimmermann Telegram. Between these two events, President Wilson thought he had no other options left. On April 2, 1917, Wilson went before Congress to request a declaration of war. Wilson said that the United States would enter the war "to vindicate the principles of peace and justice in the life of the world."

United States president Woodrow Wilson felt backed into a corner by Germany, ultimately declaring war after accessing the Zimmermann Telegram.

As stalemates seized Europe, Germany attempted to use its naval forces to progress. However, the British blockaded German ships in their harbors in an attempt to ensure that Germany could receive no imports and in the hopes that its people could be starved into submission. This plan may have worked, had the German navy not deployed U-boats, or submarines, to torpedo British supply ships. While all British ships may have been fair game, the Germans didn't care who they hit. In this attack, the Germans also sunk the ships of other countries, including vessels from the then-neutral United States. When the Germans sank the British ocean liner *Lusitania* on May 7, 1915, 128 US citizens were killed. The United States' hand had been forced: Germany was at war with the Americans, too.

In the meantime, the Russian military was facing instability. Germany was gaining traction in the east. In March 1917, the Germans signed the Treaties of Brest-Litovsk, gaining valuable territory in Poland, the Baltic States, Finland, and Ukraine by agreeing to stop their invasion of Russia. If this seemed like a victory, it was short-lived. Two groups were angered by Brest-Litovsk, and the first was in fact a group of Germans. The country's radical socialists had come to understand that the intentions of their motherland were to gain as much territory as possible—that is, imperialism. The socialists didn't support this and certainly didn't support the fact that Germany's working men were being pulled from their jobs—and dying—to fight for such a cause.

Outrage from outside of Germany, however, would come to be the empire's downfall. The Allies of the west were disgusted to see how greedy Germany was in how it dealt with defeated enemies. The United States, backed by plenty of troops and munitions, was determined to defeat Germany.

The empire's loss on all fronts was looming. At home, the German people were demonstrating against the war, which had cost the lives of six million men. In the east, the country's allies began to drop out, leaving the Germans to fight alone. And in the west, the strength of a reenergized Allied force proved too much for them to overpower.

With total defeat imminent, Germany moved to establish a new system of governance controlled by socialist leaders. In November 1918, a new constitution called for an elected president and chancellor to rule the country. After World War I had claimed ten million lives, Germany signed an armistice, or a formal agreement to stop fighting. Its new government leaders knew they would have to cede all the territory they had gained through the Treaties of Brest-Litovsk. They didn't know that their rivals would ask for further concessions.

The peace negotiations took place in Paris starting in January 1919—and the Germans weren't there. The British, French, Americans, and Italians all had representatives present, but the Germans were not invited to be a part of deciding their own fate. The

French troops leave the Rhineland after occupying Germany following Wold War I.

French were the most adamant that the Germans pay a heavy price; after all, much of the war had been fought on French soil. The French believed that the Germans should have to forfeit all of their industrial heartlands, including the Saar region and all territory west of the Rhine. Fortunately for the Germans, the British and Americans thought this punishment was too harsh. In the end, the Treaty of Versailles determined that the Germans would hand over Alsace and Lorraine to France, a pair of Prussian provinces to Poland, and three cities to Belgium. French troops would occupy the Rhineland until Germans paid $32 billion (more than $452 billion in today's money) in war reparations as a means of compensating for the damage they had inflicted and until they accepted total responsibility for starting the war. Germany had no choice but to agree to the terms.

The war that saw Germany make significant territorial gains at first ultimately cost the country greatly. The British blockade of German ports continued, and hunger broke out among the German people. A governing system that came to be known as the Weimar Republic was left with the responsibility of trying to turn around an angry, war-weary, and humiliated people.

CHAPTER THREE

The Rise of Hitler, and Germany's Dismantling

In the winter of 1919, Germany was technically a united nation, but the challenges its citizens would face after the war left the door open for years of upheaval that would ultimately lead to World War II. The German people were upset that their country had lost so much during World War I, and they were outraged at the concessions that followed. For years, they had been led to believe that they were winning battles during World War I and that they were the victims of other countries' antagonisms. Somehow, the Germans were left with less land, less economic opportunity, and the responsibility of accepting blame for starting a war that caused massive death and destruction.

The Germans were forced to accept the terms of the Treaty of Versailles on July 7, 1919. The Weimar constitution was ratified soon afterward. The

In this map from 1920, German borders have been redrawn after the end of World War I, when the country was forced to cede territories to other nations.

governmental system outlined in this constitution was quite liberal, ensuring democratic representation for a number of parties. The German people, however, would long associate the passing of the constitution with the Treaty of Versailles, which they loathed.

The first half of the 1920s in Germany was marked by infighting between various groups and a struggling economy. In the face of both the costs of war and the reparation payments the nation owed, the value of the German currency plummeted. Meanwhile, the territories momentarily gained during WWI, which had seemed so full of promise, were now ruled by other countries.

Once Germany began making amends with its former enemies, circumstances improved. German chancellor Gustav Stresemann convinced the Allies to lighten the Germans' economic debts through the Dawes Plan (1924), which also provided American loans to boost the economy. The next year, Stresemann signed the Pact of Locarno, in which Germany accepted the borders of France and Belgium and agreed to work peacefully to resolve border disputes with Poland and Czechoslovakia. Ultimately, Germany was invited back into the League of Nations, an organization founded in 1920 to pursue cooperation between countries. As Germany's international standing improved, the rebellions throughout the country died down.

However, the world's economic implosion, which would come to be known as the Great Depression, took the Germans off course. The US stock market crashed in 1929, and as a result, the Germans were no longer receiving loans from the Americans. The German bank system failed, and unemployment skyrocketed. The angst that had overtaken the country a decade before resurfaced. During elections in the 1930s, extremist parties began to gain ground. By 1932, the leader of the National Socialist German Workers' Party, also known as the Nazi Party, would have 37 percent of the popular vote. His name was Adolf Hitler.

The Rise of Adolf Hitler

Hitler may not have had the opportunity to rise to power if Germany had not been in such a state of flux. However, the people were still angry over the country's defeat in WWI, and when Hitler blamed the Jewish people, he gave the masses permission to target these groups. Hitler clawed his way up the political ranks and was named chancellor in 1933; at the same time, opposition parties were being systematically oppressed, and the Weimar Republic effectively folded. It wouldn't be long before Hitler's primary ambition would be made clear: he wanted to expand German territory so as to gain more living space for the so-called Aryan race, light-skinned people whom he considered superior to all others.

This idea was not new. As early as the 1880s, German geographer Friedrich Ratzel had advocated for expanding German territory. Ratzel adopted the philosophy that successful civilizations migrated to new areas, adapting to the geographic circumstances. He argued that this would allow the people to naturally continue spreading and adapting to different circumstances. This concept, when applied in Germany, was known as Lebensraum. It further stated that

Adolf Hitler, pictured here at a 1934 rally in Nuremberg, took advantage of an unstable German government to promote the rise of the Nazi Party. Hitler became chancellor in 1933.

Germans should gain their living space from the east—where Russia was located—and colonize it by establishing peasant farms.

Hitler was familiar with Ratzel's philosophy of Lebensraum, and he studied it further when he was incarcerated from 1924 to 1925, during which period he wrote his violently racist political manifesto, *Mein Kampf* (*My Struggle*). Hitler also read the works of a Munich professor of geography, Karl Haushofer, who observed that Germany was in an unfavorable geographical situation due to its limited resources of food and raw materials. Hitler used all this as ammunition to expand—and invade.

Hitler's stance gained traction among many segments of the German population: middle-class Germans who had been negatively impacted by the Great Depression, those still angry about the Treaty of Versailles, those who feared Communism, and those who were attracted to his nationalist message, which asserted Germany's right to return to a high standing in the international hierarchy.

Once Hitler and the Nazi Party had formally secured power, the chancellor set about rebuilding the German military and reviving the economy. Despite the fact that Hitler was taking a dictatorial approach to government, many Germans were happy with his leadership because rebuilding the military led to the creation of many jobs. Around this same time came the passage of the Nuremberg Laws, which officially deprived Jews of German citizenship. In promoting

German nationalism and unity, Hitler depicted Germans as the master race, superior to Jews and Slavs.

In light of his growing power, Hitler attempted to test the western powers' alliance. He announced that Germany would ignore the borders outlined in the Pact of Locarno. Germany reannexed and remilitarized the Rhineland, which had been occupied by Allied troops until mid-1930. Although this was a serious violation of the Treaty of Versailles, the Allied powers did nothing to thwart Hitler's movements, mostly because they could not agree on a plan of action. Hitler spent 1936 developing his own alliances with Austria and Italy, developing what would become known as the Axis Powers.

On September 1, 1939, news of Germany's march through Poland spread around the world. Hitler's initial alliances were with Austria and Italy.

By 1938, Hitler had taken over Austria entirely. Military or geographic strategy does not seem to have been the primary motivation for this move; more than anything, it was symbolic: Hitler was advocating a return to the state of mind of the mid- to late-1800s. Expanding German territory to include Austria would restore the previous borders.

Hitler's next move was a strategic test of the Allied powers. He moved on to the Sudetenland region of Czechoslovakia, which had an ethnic population of German-speaking people. Hitler believed that these people belonged with their fellow Germans. In the Munich Agreement (1938), the western powers let Hitler take the Sudetenland and proposed that other Czechoslovakian regions with a significant Sudeten German population should have the opportunity to vote as to whether they wished to join the German state. Hitler was warned that, should he attempt to control any other parts of Czechoslovakia, the Allied powers would fight back. He called their bluff. In March 1939, he and his troops invaded the remainder of Czechoslovakia, but the Allied powers did nothing to stop it.

World War II

Tensions rose as Hitler militarized and expanded Germany through the latter half of the 1930s. It was Hitler's desire to annex Poland that ultimately sparked World War II. Channeling the philosophy of Lebensraum, Hitler was seeking new territories in which to establish the German people and their supposedly superior Aryan race. Poland was a large and agriculturally rich country in which German peasant farms could be fruitfully established—assuring their cultural dominance was secured in the process.

German Expansion

Nonetheless, Hitler took a realistic approach to annexing Poland: he knew he would need help. Hitler sought out the aid of Joseph Stalin, the leader of the Soviet Union, despite the fact that, when it came to politics, they were ideologically opposed. They negotiated the German-Soviet Nonaggression Pact of August 1939, in which they agreed that their countries would divide Poland between them. Hitler's military utilized blitzkrieg tactics in its assault of Poland; the Luftwaffe (air force) conducted relentless air attacks, while tanks plowed across Polish territory. Germans also utilized strategic tactics to prevent Poles from communicating with one another and obtaining needed supplies. Bolstered by the Russian invasion from the east, the Germans took Warsaw on September 27, 1939, after which the Russians and Germans divided up the land, as planned.

Hitler had entered Polish territory assuming that the Allied powers wouldn't resist his march through Europe. This time, he was wrong. Two days after German troops entered Poland, Great Britain and France declared war.

Two German aircraft are pictured over the London Docklands in the fall of 1940. The German Luftwaffe was a key component of Adolf Hitler's military scheme throughout World War II.

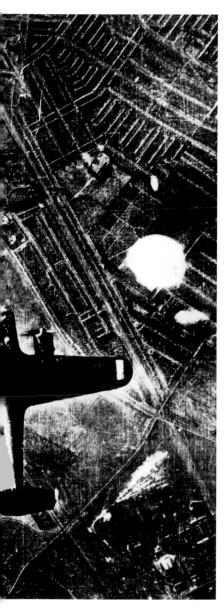

As the western powers mobilized, Hitler continued with his plan. In Poland, he had begun to enact what the Nazis called "the final solution of the Jewish question," forcing Jews to wear a yellow Star of David affixed to their clothes, while stripping them of their property and belongings. Meanwhile, the German military wove through the Baltic States, invading Estonia, Latvia, and Lithuania. They acquired Denmark as a means to reach Norway, which was of strategic importance because its ports provided access to the North Atlantic and could open up trade opportunities for Germany. Having taken over Norway, the Germans could gain access to the mineral-rich mines of Sweden.

Belgium and the Netherlands would become Hitler's stepping stones as he moved toward France. This invasion would

THE PORT OF HAMBURG

Valuable resources were lost throughout Europe as a result of World War II. Individual countries, including Germany, ultimately ceded a great deal of territory, and the destruction caused by countless battles and bombings was overwhelming.

The Port of Hamburg, located in north Germany, was bombed by the Allies in 1943. This was devastating for Germany, as Hamburg was—and still is—Germany's largest port and had been nicknamed the Gateway to the World. The port was founded in the year 1189 CE and was hugely important in allowing Germany to engage in transatlantic trade, particularly after the discovery of the Americas. The branching Elbe River provided the ideal setting for warehouse and shipment facilities.

The Allies knew how crucial this port was for the Germans and undertook a series of air raids in July 1943 that lasted for eight days and seven nights. The Hamburg shipyards lost fleets of ships, and the city itself was largely destroyed. The air raids, known as Operation Gomorrah, killed 42,600 people and caused nearly one million Germans to flee the city. Estimates found that the raids destroyed 183 large factories—more than one-third of all such facilities in the city—and 4,118 smaller factories (nearly half of Hamburg's total). Local transportation systems were entirely disrupted and would not resume for a long time. German armaments production, in particular, was severely stunted as a result of the bombing, making the offensive a pivotal victory for the Allies.

A BETRAYED RUSSIA

If Adolf Hitler had never betrayed his alliance with Russian leader Joseph Stalin, Germany might have not been defeated in World War II. At the very least, the Allied victory would have been even more difficult.

hold great symbolic significance for the German people. France and Germany's history dated to the 1870s, when, through war with the French, Germany was first united. About fifty years later, France would be one of countries to lead the way in defeating Germany in World War I. Seeking revenge for the Treaty of Versailles was among Hitler's top agenda items, so France was an important target. The Germans forced the French to surrender in their capital city of Paris less than two weeks after entering the country.

Another Allied power—Great Britain—was the next target. The Battle of Britain was fought through a series of air raids in mid-1940 that pitted the Luftwaffe against the Royal Air Force. London suffered severe damage, but Germany was unable to secure a total takeover, due to the strength of the Royal Air Force and the American aid arriving in British ports. Hitler changed course.

It was hard to believe that the Soviets and Germans would ever completely align with one another, given how ideologically different the two countries' leaders were. The alliance had served both countries well in the invasion of Poland, but by June 1941, Hitler turned his troops toward the east. Hitler was greedy for more land, but he also had other reasons for setting his sights on the Russians: the Soviets had annexed the Baltic states of Lithuania, Latvia, and Estonia, previously conquered by Hitler. What's more, the two were now disputing who could claim strategic Balkan oil fields.

Germany's invasion of Russia was backed by three million troops and came from three directions: through Finland in the north, Poland in the west, and Romania in the south. Employing the same blitzkrieg tactics that had served them well previously, Hitler and the German military captured 2.5 million Soviet troops in less than six months. Hitler, however, would not advance all the way to the Russian capital of Moscow, as the brutal winter stopped the troops from moving forward.

Headway for the Allied Powers

The German offensive against Russia, combined with the Americans' entrance into World War II, would spell the beginning of the end for Hitler and the Germans. The Japanese bombing of Pearl Harbor spurred the United States to join the war on the side of the Allies, which provided much-needed manpower and supplies. Initially, the Axis powers would hold off the Allies in North Africa, but Germany remained focused on Russia, particularly the Soviet city of Stalingrad.

With its attention split, and its Italian ally crumbling, a much-weakened Germany was bracing itself for defeat on two fronts. In June 1944, a massive Allied invasion came ashore at Normandy, in what would come to be known as the D-Day landings. Almost two hundred thousand Allied troops landed on the beaches of northern France, defeating the German forces who had been attempting to block entrance. The Allies quickly advanced across France toward Germany. Meanwhile, a resurgent Soviet military was headed toward the German borders.

By late February 1945, the Soviets were approaching Berlin while British and American forces closed in on the Rhine River. Two months later, on April 30, 1945, Hitler committed suicide, and on May 7, 1945, Hitler's successor, Admiral Karl Donitz, surrendered to American commander General Dwight D. Eisenhower. The following day, Donitz surrendered to the Soviets.

More than 35 million Europeans died during World War II, including 4.5 million German soldiers, an unknown number of German civilians, and more than 6 million Jews. In perhaps the greatest horror of the most devastating war the world had ever seen, Jewish people from throughout Europe had been imprisoned in German extermination camps, where millions of men, women, and children were systematically starved and murdered. Gas chambers were built for the express purpose of killing large numbers of Jews, solely because Nazi ideology considered them ethnically inferior to whites, and specifically to

Nordic and Germanic peoples. Slavs, Roma (Gypsies), homosexuals, and people with alleged mental disabilities were also interned and murdered in these camps. This systematic, state-sponsored genocide would come to be known as the Holocaust, and during the Nuremberg trials of 1945–1946, German military and political leaders would be prosecuted for crimes against humanity, among other charges, for their role in the creation and operation of these camps.

Hitler's grand ambitions to expand German territory had been successful for a time, but he had left millions dead and Europe devastated in his wake, and he ultimately failed to secure more land for his country. Instead, Germany would be split into occupied zones, and in 1945, its future as a nation was more uncertain than it had been for decades.

Starving slave laborers, including future Nazi-hunter Elie Wiesel (*second row from bottom, seventh from left*), greet the US 80th Army Division, who have arrived at Buchenwald concentration camp in 1945 to liberate them.

CHAPTER FOUR

From Division to the Toppling of the Berlin Wall

As after World War I, Germany's fate would be decided without its leaders' input. The Potsdam Conference, held near Berlin from July 17 through August 2, 1945, was attended by Soviet premier Joseph Stalin, United States president Harry S. Truman, and two prime ministers of Great Britain: first, Winston Churchill, then his successor, Clement Attlee. The goal was to plan for a postwar Europe.

German reparations were a primary topic of discussion. War reparations are payments in the form of money or goods made to other countries to cover damage inflicted or injuries experienced during a war. The leaders at the Potsdam Conference determined that Germany should pay the Allies approximately $23 billion (about $312.7 billion in today's money) in the form of machinery and manufacturing plants.

After World War II, Germany was divided into four occupation zones, overseen by the British, Americans, French, and Soviets. The capital of Berlin was divided into eastern and western territories.

Germany also paid back other countries in the form of forced labor. About four million German prisoners of war and civilians worked as laborers in the Soviet Union, France, the United Kingdom, Belgium, and parts of Germany overseen by the United States.

Stalin insisted that the land east of the Oder and Neisse rivers be returned to Poland. Polish borders were also redrawn to include part of former East Prussia, where Germans had been living. Germans were made to leave Czechoslovakia and Hungary, and millions were forced to relocate.

Postwar Occupation and Economic Recovery

Months earlier, at the Yalta Conference in February 1945, a plan had been developed for the oversight of German territory. Germany was to be divided into four occupation zones, each overseen by one of four Allied powers: the United States, Britain, France, and the Soviet Union. However, it quickly became clear that the western Allied powers would work together, while the Soviets would govern independently.

The overseeing countries were charged with several responsibilities. First, they were to provide food, housing, and medical care to the people under their charge. More broadly, they were to move toward the disarmament of Germany, the denazification of the country, and the rebuilding of the German economy. While Adolf Hitler had relied upon war and military efforts to boost the country's wealth, the new German economy would emphasize agriculture and other nonmilitary industries. All in attendance at Yalta agreed that the priority was to ensure that Germany would not be capable of preparing for a new war. The western Allied powers would also emphasize democratizing, decentralizing, and deindustrializing the country.

Upon returning to the United States, Truman gave a radio address to the American people, invoking hope for the future of the German nation. "I have just returned from Berlin, the city from which the Germans intended to rule the world," he said. "We are going to do what we can to make Germany over into a decent nation, so that it may eventually work its way from the economic chaos it has brought upon itself, back into a place in the civilized world."

The geographical dilemma caused by the division of German between four countries was the location of Berlin: it was in the northeast corner of the country, in the territory designated for the Soviet Union. It was determined that, while the Soviets would control that region as a whole, Berlin would be divided into four occupation zones (as Austria and its capital, Vienna). The conference in Potsdam was less than friendly, as most countries in attendance were acting in their own self-interest, and the western Allied powers were leery of Stalin's intentions. The management of Berlin would foment greater international division in the years to come.

Rebuilding Germany

After the war, the western powers focused on rebuilding Germany's economy. New democratic governments and a range of political parties were being formed.

The Soviets, however, took a different approach. Led by a wartime hero, Marshal Georgy Zhukov, the

Soviets set up their German territory as a Communist puppet state. This entailed a fundamental shift in East Germans' way of life. The Soviets nationalized the banks and factories, while redistributing private agricultural land into collective farms, a method of governance that was Communist in spirit. The Soviets also stripped the German territory of many of its assets: they dismantled entire German factories and sent the equipment and raw materials to the Soviet Union.

While the Soviets and western powers had long disagreed about how to properly govern a country, they did so as relatively neutral neighbors for several years. Slowly, though, countries such as the United States began a campaign to prevent the spread of Communism. This led to what was known as the Cold War era, which would last roughly from the late 1940s until the late 1980s. During this period, physical conflict never occurred between the United States and the Soviet Union, but ideological and political disagreement dominated the international conversation, separating the Soviets and their Communist counterparts from the western world.

The Cold War

In the winter of 1946, Great Britain's Winston Churchill gave a speech in which he coined the term "Iron Curtain" to describe the way in which Communist-controlled countries were isolated from democratic nations in the west. Then, in June 1947, the United States implemented the Marshall Plan, which offered aid to devastated countries in Europe to rebuild their economies. Doing so also provided a larger market for American exports. The western German zones received a combined $1 billion in aid from the United States, catapulting these territories far above the level of economic opportunity and standard of living of their East German counterparts. Stalin did not take well to the program, claiming that the western Allies were disregarding the agreements of the Potsdam Conference.

On June 27, 1948, the Soviets cut off ground access to West Berlin, in direct violation of the Potsdam Conference's Declaration on Germany. Stalin confirmed that this was an attempt to thwart the Marshall Plan. With the Iron Curtain effectively lowered, the Allied powers were unable to send shipments of food, fuel, and medicine to inhabitants of the western-controlled areas of Berlin. Starvation seemed imminent. In response, the Allies pooled the resources they had used in battle during World War II and readied for an event known as the Berlin airlift, during which the Allies sent more than two hundred seventy thousand relief flights stocked with supplies to the region. In total, 2.3 million tons of food, fuel, and other essentials arrived in West Berlin. Meanwhile, relations between the east and west were worsening.

Separate States

On July 1, 1948, the western powers decided they should draft a constitution for a federal state comprised

of the three territories in Germany they oversaw. This territory would be known as the Federal Republic of Germany (FRG), or in German, Bundesrepublik Deutschland. Less than a year later, the Basic Law, or Grundgesetz, was formally enacted. Under this constitution, Germans were afforded a number of civil rights, and a federal government and national judiciary were established.

The Soviets responded in October of 1949 by establishing the German Democratic Republic (GDR), a Communist satellite state with its own constitution and legislative body. The western Allies refused to recognize the GDR as a sovereign state. While the two territories within the former Germany were each developing into independent and more structured nations, the division between them grew.

Both new nations were attaining some success. The democratic FRG

The Soviet Union cut off ground entrance to West Berlin, which led to the Berlin airlift. The Allied powers utilized airplanes to send provisions to the citizens of West Berlin.

leaned early on the leadership of West Germany's first chancellor, Konrad Adenauer, who was able to gain the loyalty of the German people while earning the trust of the western world. Under his leadership, and supported by the aid entering the country via the Marshall Plan, the economy flourished. This period of recovery in West Germany during the 1950s was appropriately known as the "economic miracle." A social welfare system was developed, entitling workers and retirees to a range of benefits that enabled them to participate in the growing national economy. West Germany also became a major exporter to nations throughout Europe and to the United States. Diplomatically, West Germany achieved international success when it was granted entrance into the North Atlantic Treaty Organization (NATO).

In East Germany, most of the power was concentrated with Communist Walter Ulbricht, who assisted in issuing the Five-Year Plan. This focused on redistributing agricultural lands and significantly increasing the output of factories. It would never match the success of its western neighbor, but East Germany did become a leader among nations to the east of the Iron Curtain. In response to West Germany's entrance into NATO, the Soviet Union developed the Warsaw Treaty Organization, or Warsaw Pact, a military alliance of Communist states. Meanwhile, East Germany and West Germany continued in their refusal to acknowledge each other's sovereignty.

The Berlin Wall

Tensions would heighten when Nikita Khrushchev became the new Soviet premier in 1958. Khrushchev claimed that the western powers were abusing their power in West Berlin to conduct activities against the GDR. He wanted them out. Khrushchev said that if the western occupants would not leave West Berlin, allowing the whole city to be "free" and demilitarized, he would sign a peace treaty with the GDR that might threaten the occupation of West Berlin.

Khrushchev and the Soviet leadership were also responding to a disconcerting trend: millions of East Germans were leaving for West Germany in search of greater economic opportunity and more political freedom. In 1953 alone, four hundred thousand East Germans defected to move west. The number of defectors only increased as the GDR's secret police force, known as the Stasi, became more powerful and oppressive. Many of the region's most promising young citizens were leaving the country.

However, the western Allies knew that, should they withdraw, West Berlin would most likely come under Soviet control and a Communist system would be put in place. They did not agree to Khrushchev's terms.

In June 1961, Khrushchev met with the new American president, John F. Kennedy, in the hopes of resolving the Berlin crisis. Kennedy had previously shared his thoughts with American economist and political theorist Walt Rostow, saying: "Khrushchev is losing East Germany. He cannot let that happen. If East Germany goes, so will Poland and all of eastern Europe. He will have to do something to stop the flow of refugees—perhaps a wall. And we won't be able to prevent it. I can hold the Alliance together to defend West Berlin but I cannot act to keep East Berlin open."

In their meeting, Khrushchev told Kennedy that he would allow the western powers to sign a peace treaty with the Soviets without explicitly recognizing the GDR's sovereignty. Kennedy, for his part, told the Russian premier that the Americans were prepared to go to war to safeguard their interests in West Berlin; he would, however, allow the Soviets to do as they pleased in the eastern part of the city.

The people of East Germany were in a state of "gate-closing panic" (a term adapted from the

Construction of the Berlin Wall began on August 13, 1961. The wall
divided East and West Berlin.

From Division to the Toppling of the Berlin Wall   **63**

BUILDING THE WALL

The Berlin Wall was built because the US and Soviet governments disagreed about the Americans' presence in Berlin. The barbed-wire fence that first drew the physical separation was built overnight. It was later replaced by a concrete wall and other barriers to crossing, including dog runs, trenches, and watchtowers.

German *Torschlusspanik*) when they learned that their access to the prosperous West Berlin might soon come to an end. Twenty thousand East Germans fled the GDR in June, followed by thirty thousand more in July. Members of the Warsaw Pact met in early August 1961 and voted to construct a wall dividing West and East Berlin.

While dividing the country with a physical barrier was not part of the initial intention of the attendees of the Potsdam Conference, the Berlin Wall was seen as a sufficient resolution among many on the international stage. Kennedy felt relieved; it seemed Khrushchev would leave West Berlin alone. Privately to his aides, Kennedy said: "Why would Khrushchev put up a wall if he really intended to seize West Berlin? There wouldn't be any need of a wall if he occupied the whole city. This is his way out of his predicament. It's not a very nice solution, but a wall is a hell of a lot better than a war." Construction of the wall began on August 13, 1961.

Walter Ulbricht led East Germany to a degree of economic success. He focused on the redistribution of agricultural lands and factory output.

While those in the international community were congratulating themselves for avoiding more destructive conflict, those in East and West Germany had different feelings about the wall's construction. West German chancellor Adenauer had thought that the FRG's close alignment with the western Allies would ultimately promote the reunification of Germany. He was distraught to learn they had other intentions. In a speech on August 18, Adenauer exclaimed: "To the German people must be returned the right, which is refused to no other people in the world, freely to establish a government of its own enjoying the legitimate task of speaking, acting, and making decisions for all of Germany."

On the other side of the wall, East German leader Ulbricht saw the building of the wall as the final step in legitimizing the GDR. On August 25, 1961, Ulbricht stated, "Herr Adenauer has determined with sadness that his revanchist German policy has collapsed at the Brandenburg Gate. The great heel of history cannot be turned back. Herr Adenauer has had to accept the fact that the GDR is here to stay." However, even Ulbricht saw a divided Germany as a short-term arrangement. He maintained the Soviets' stance that East Germany would one day be a standalone Communist nation.

In the same speech, Ulbricht redeclared his vision:

Thanks to the political clarity, and to the capabilities and energies of the citizens of the GDR, we will be able to create the preconditions for a time when Berlin,

Konrad Adenauer was the first chancellor of West Germany. Adenauer was able to connect with both the German people and leaders abroad.

our Berlin, will become the capital of Germany in its
entirety, a Germany in which there is no militarism, no
imperialism, and no black-brown-yellow dictatorship,
but only the working class, which in alliance with the
farmers and all other peace-loving forces is able to
shape the destiny of the new Germany.

Outside Influence

However, with reluctance on both sides, Germany
forged ahead as a divided country under the continued
influence of foreign nations. Kennedy, who had been
elected president of the United States in 1960, had
committed to opposing the Soviet political system, but
he also stated in his inaugural address in January 1961
that he was open to negotiation. "Let us never negotiate
out of fear," he said. "But let us never fear to negotiate.
Let both sides explore what problems unite us instead
of belaboring those problems which divide us."

This resolve was put to the test in 1962, when
it was confirmed that the Soviets had placed nuclear
missiles in Cuba, the United States' close neighbor with
whom relations were tense. Despite this escalation,
Kennedy and Khrushchev were able to come to an
agreement that marked the very beginning of the
"thaw" of Cold War tensions. In 1968, the United
States, the Soviet Union, Great Britain, and other
nations signed the Treaty on the Non-Proliferation of
Nuclear Weapons, agreeing not to help other countries
attain such weapons.

To West Germans and Adenauer, Kennedy's behavior seemed to reinforce the idea that the western Allies' intentions in West Germany were not focused on reunification but on maintaining *détente*—that is, a period of improved relations among countries during a time of political conflict. Kennedy told Adenauer in no uncertain terms that West Germany didn't have other options.

East German leader Ulbricht was upset. He recalled Khrushchev's initial promise that the Soviets would sign a peace treaty with East Germany; this had never come to pass. Ulbricht was increasingly concerned over the dangers that West Germany's alliance with France might present to East Germans. Khrushchev acknowledged Ulbricht's concern but didn't make any moves to formally assist East Germany, instead expressing how encouraged he felt by peace negotiations with the West.

Improving Relations

In many ways, the fate of the two Germanys seemed to be decided far outside their own borders. However, peace between the nations was beginning to seem possible. In 1971, West German chancellor Willy Brandt was awarded the Nobel Peace Prize for being a "European Bridge-Builder." Among Brandt's accomplishments were West Germany's signing of the Nuclear Non-Proliferation Treaty and agreeing to a nonviolence pact with the Soviet Union. He was also instrumental in an agreement with Poland, in which West Germany formally acknowledged and accepted the new international borders established after World War II. At the time, the Soviet Union and West Germany also agreed to build an oil pipeline between the two nations. Brandt's work laid the foundation for the 1971 Four Power accord on Berlin, which improved travel and communication between West and East Germany and allowed families to more easily visit relatives on the other side of the Berlin Wall.

A pivotal moment came in 1972, when West and East Germany established the Grundvertrag, or Basic Treaty. For the first time, the FRG and GDR recognized each other as sovereign states. They vowed to respect the other's authority and independence. This paved the way for both German states to be recognized by the international community—a huge victory for East Germany, which had long lacked legitimacy—and to ultimately be admitted to the United Nations.

Egon Bahr, a West German politician, is often quoted by historians to reflect the mood of the two German nations at the time: "Previously, we have had no relations," Bahr said. "[Now] we will have bad ones, and this is progress. It will be a long time before we have better ones."

East Germany benefitted economically from the new arrangement. As West Germans crossed the border into the GDR, they utilized the more valuable West German currency and paid the necessary fees, such as highway tolls. Still, East Germany was struggling:

A West Berliner greets his mother at a border crossing in Berlin on November 2, 1964. GDR pensioners were permitted to visit family on this date for the first time since the Berlin Wall was built.

it was later found to have been dishonest toward its citizens regarding the country's economic situation. As East Germany poured its resources into industrial production to focus on its role as an exporter, the country's infrastructure deteriorated and a housing shortage resulted.

Mikhail Gorbachev became the general secretary of the Soviet Union—also known as the USSR—in 1985 and arrived on the scene with plans to democratize the country's political system and decentralize the economy. He was largely recognized for implementing policies of *glasnost* (openness) and *perestroika* (restructuring) in his attempt to rejuvenate the failing Soviet economy.

The goal of openness led to cultural changes in the Soviet nation, as freedom of expression became more widespread and the country's media began to provide more honest coverage. Changes to the economy came more slowly, as government bureaucrats hesitated to loosen the reins of control over their nation's economy.

Gorbachev was instrumental in "thawing" the Cold War by cultivating more productive relationships with western powers, namely the United States. In December 1987, Gorbachev and US president Ronald Reagan signed an agreement to destroy some of their nuclear missiles.

Gorbachev used these successes as a springboard to promote a new era of governance among other nations in the Soviet bloc. East Germany pushed back, even though many Communist regimes were being replaced. Democratically elected, non-Communist governments arose in Poland, Hungary, and Czechoslovakia—and later, the same would happen in East Germany.

Previously, these and other countries had been under the purview of the Soviet Union. The Brezhnev Doctrine, a Soviet foreign policy outlined in 1968, had limited the sovereignty of Communist satellite states. It had also given the Soviet Union the power to intervene should any individual country appear to be compromising the cohesiveness of the Soviet bloc. However, given the changes many of these countries were now undergoing, Gorbachev agreed to withdraw troops.

In East Germany, Gorbachev pushed for the same reform. He attended East Germany's fortieth anniversary celebrations on October 6–7, 1989, and instead of supporting the course set by its then-leader Erich Honecker, he promoted his message of "democratization, openness, socialist legality, and the free development of all peoples and their equal inclusion in [their country's] affairs." He effectively told the people of East Germany that, if they should revolt against the policies and procedures of their government, he would not intervene to suppress their efforts.

Perhaps more surprisingly, Gorbachev approved of the prospect of a reunited Germany, even though it would mean that the reunited country would become a member of a group that the Soviet Union had long considered an adversary, the North Atlantic Treaty Organization. Gorbachev assumed that democracy and socialism could go hand in hand, which proved to be untrue in this case and led to the dismantling of the Soviet Union and ultimately a decline in Soviet power and influence in Eastern Europe.

Gorbachev's intervention into German affairs is the primary reason the Berlin Wall came down without bloodshed. That's why, in 1990, Gorbachev was awarded the Nobel Peace Prize "for his leading role in the peace process which today characterizes important parts of the international community."

Soviet leader Mikhail Gorbachev was instrumental in improving east-west relations and in the dismantling of the Berlin Wall.

From the East German perspective, perhaps the greatest drawback of this new arrangement was the fact that citizens of both nations were increasingly interacting with one another. Those from the dictator-controlled east were hearing and seeing more and more about the opportunities in the democratic west. East Germany had enacted internal policies to limit these types of interactions, such as raising visa fees for visitors and forbidding certain East German citizens from personal contact with those west of the wall. This policy relaxed over time, and by the 1980s, it was easier than ever to visit relatives across the border; tens of thousands of citizens were even granted permission to emigrate to West Germany. In exchange, the west provided large bank loans to East Germany.

Some parties in West Germany were unhappy with this situation. They opposed the East German political system and struggled to see why their own government should legitimize the dictatorship on the other side of the wall, where free elections were not allowed. They were also disturbed that the East German government allowed its guards along the Berlin Wall to shoot fleeing citizens. In 1987, after a change of leadership in both nations—with Erich Honecker now leading the east and Helmut Kohl as chancellor in the west—Honecker was received in West Germany with full state honors. It seemed that West Germany had fully accepted its neighboring state.

Reunification

If East Germany's presence on the international stage was improving, the morale among its citizenry was declining. While Honecker presented an image of stability, East Germans knew it to be a façade. This opinion was particularly strong in the younger generation of East Germans, who had taken advantage of the opportunity to travel to West Germany. The benefits of democracy were astounding: higher-quality goods, a currency valued outside the country's own borders, and freedom of expression.

The events that ultimately led to the reunification of Germany began mostly outside German borders: citizens in Communist countries throughout the east were pushing for change. When Mikhail Gorbachev took over as Soviet leader in the late 1980s, he proposed and enforced several reforms that startled the citizens of the Soviet Union. Other eastern nations could not ignore this shift. Gorbachev promoted perestroika, or restructuring, of the Communist-controlled government in the Soviet Union and suggested the same approach to Honecker and East Germany. Honecker vehemently disagreed, stating: "The young man [Gorbachev] has been making policy for only a year, and already he wants to take on more than he can chew!"

As the Soviet Union changed, the press was less controlled by the government, agricultural reforms

FROM DIVISION TO UNITY

Much of German history prior to the 1930s was focused on the country's attempts to acquire more territory. The final border change, however, was not about an external territory gain. With the falling of the Berlin Wall and the reunification of Germany, the country's outer borders did not change. Rather, the long-divided nation had become one once again.

For decades, West Germany (*yellow*) and East Germany were separate nations with different ideologies guiding their governments.

The Berlin Wall was a guarded concrete barrier physically dividing West and East Berlin from 1961 to 1989. The Berlin Wall was more than 87 miles (140 kilometers) long. There were nine border crossings between East and West Berlin. The wall evolved over time, in an attempt to make it less passable. An area known as the "death strip" contained trenches that vehicles could not pass through.

In 1989, the Berlin Wall was torn down, making way for a united German nation where citizens were able to move about the country as they wished.

and economic cooperatives were encouraged, and democratic participation in decision making became—to some extent—the norm. Honecker continued to push back. The East German media, however, began to highlight the real experience of living in East Germany, despite Honecker's ban on such content. The *Neues Deutschland* newspaper, for example, published articles about rising alcoholism, homelessness, and food shortages in the Soviet Union.

Honecker would not risk an ideological separation with the Soviet Union, but he and his colleagues developed an alternative stance to help the people of East Germany understand their intentions. Put simply, Honecker said that socialist nations may agree about some elements of governance, but each individual country needed to decide what was best for it. Maybe the Soviet Union was making changes, he explained, but that didn't mean that East Germany had to follow suit.

Many of Honecker's citizens felt otherwise. In the late 1980s, activist groups increased their presence in East Germany. They voiced their desire for more political participation, greater religious freedom, and governmental involvement in cleaning up East Germany's polluted environment.

West Germany took notice of the unsettling series of events happening on the other side of the wall. It encouraged East German leadership to be more tolerant and generous toward their citizens. West Germany also iterated that its intent was not to "depopulate" East Germany and suggested that Honecker's government could benefit from again loosening travel restrictions. In 1988, 6.7 million East Germans visited the west, while thirty thousand individuals were given permission to emigrate there. However, tearing down the Berlin Wall was not plausible, according to Honecker, who said in January 1989, "The Wall will remain as long as the reasons for its presence have not been eliminated. It will still be there in 50 and even 100 years." Nonetheless, by mid-June of 1989, Honecker relaxed policy again: East German border guards were no longer permitted to shoot fleeing citizens.

Relations between the citizens and the East German government remained tense. Advocacy groups, including some that began in the Lutheran and Roman Catholic Church communities, began to more closely monitor government activities. Such groups monitored the statewide municipal elections of May 1989 and shared irregularities with the public. Meanwhile, enthusiasm was growing for reform, such as that which was occurring in Hungary and Poland.

West German leaders found themselves questioning how to continue relations with East Germany. Chancellor Kohl's chief policy advisor, Horst Teltschik, explained the approach they took in this way: "We have recognized the existence of the GDR as a separate state, and in this sense we must also take into account its existence as a state in any future solution. For us,

East German border guards stand at a section of the Berlin Wall that has been pulled down by demonstrators on November 11, 1989.

the German question is not primarily a matter of seeking a territorial solution … Now the question is one of harmonizing German goals and desires with developments throughout Europe." Meanwhile, Kohl had invited Gorbachev to West Germany to strengthen ties with the Soviet Union and the reformed Hungarian and Polish governments.

The final steps toward the fall of the Berlin Wall began when the Hungarian government began to remove barbed-wire fences along the Austrian border. As a result, Czechoslovakia also became an exit route for those looking to leave East Germany. The exodus was significant, yet Honecker tried to pretend it wasn't happening. In the autumn of 1989, Gorbachev pushed for liberalization during a visit to the GDR, and over seventy thousand East German citizens began a demonstration calling for reform; the Honecker regime had ended.

Günter Schabowski, a member of the East German politburo—the group of senior party members—was forced to come to terms with the people's demands after seven hundred fifty thousand demonstrators in several cities protested their discontent with the travel policy. On November 9, 1989, Schabowski announced a further easing of restrictions on immigration to West Germany, adding that the new policy would be in effect immediately. Citizens gathered quickly, ordering the border guards to allow them to cross. East Germans were met on the other side by cheering West Berliners, and they celebrated together. Over the next week, bulldozers created ten more border openings along the barrier. The Berlin Wall had fallen.

CHAPTER FIVE

One Country's Struggle to Come Together

T he fall of the Berlin Wall symbolized the final stage in a reunification that had taken decades to achieve. The last formal steps toward democracy took place in December 1990, with the first free, fair, and democratic election in Germany since the Weimar era.

Elections and Treaties

Incumbent Helmut Kohl, who had been serving as chancellor of West Germany since 1982, ran against Oskar Lafontaine. During the campaign, Lafontaine embraced a slow and patient transition to reunification. Kohl, however, asked East Germans to immediately adopt a new political and economic structure in order to herald in an era of "abundance and prosperity."

Opposite: East Germans line up outside a Leipzig polling station on March 18, 1990, to vote in the all-Germany free election.

Former West German chancellor Helmut Kohl was reelected in 1990 as the chancellor of a reunited Germany. He voiced plans for a quick process of integration.

Kohl was reelected chancellor, having effectively connected with those East Germans ready to dismantle the socialist economy. (In 1991, Kohl appointed up-and-coming politician Angela Merkel to his cabinet. Merkel is considered a protégé of Kohl's and, as of 2018, had been serving as the chancellor of Germany since 2005.) However, particularly in the year that followed, former East German politicians were relegated to second-class participants. Only about one-third of representatives from the East German parliament were invited to participate in the all-German assembly, and even then, only as nonvoting members.

East Germans still supported Kohl, however. Economist Rüdiger Frank, who grew up in East Germany, has offered his perspective as to why this was the case:

> Freedom of travel, real money, and all the things you could buy for it—that's what they wanted ... And Kohl said, "This is what I'm going to give you." He was a man whom many East Germans trusted. All the other politicians, they might have had loftier political goals and more balanced approaches, but that's not what the majority cared about. They had heard enough about dreams and ideals, about justice, equality and a land of plenty that was to come someday in the future. They wanted something real, and they wanted it now. Kohl promised to deliver exactly that.

In short, East Germans were ready for change. Following the dismantling of the Berlin Wall in late 1989, the East and West German governments signed an agreement on May 18, 1990, to unify their economies. Then, on October 3, 1990, a unification treaty joined East and West Germany into a single nation, with Berlin as its capital. (Much of the German government's operations, however, would remain in the former West German capital of Bonn for many years to come.) The treaty also affirmed that the once-divided nations would act in accordance with the same federal constitution. At last, on March 15, 1991, the Final Settlement with Respect to Germany, also known as the Two Plus Four Treaty, was signed by East and West Germany, as well as the Soviet Union, the United States, Great Britain, and France—all the international powers that had divided up control of, and occupied, the German nation following World War II. With its passage, Germany had become a sovereign nation once again, giving it the right to belong to foreign alliances.

The text of the treaty declared that it had come

The Final Settlement with Respect to Germany, which was signed on March 15, 1991, gave Germany status as a sovereign nation again.

THE POLISH BORDER

The Final Settlement with Respect to Germany addressed borders outside of German territory, as well. By signing the treaty—first as separate German sovereign states, and later as a united nation—Germany agreed to accept the international borders that had been in place since the conclusion of World War II, including the Germany-Poland border: "The united Germany has no territorial claims whatsoever against other states and shall not assert any in the future." The treaty also declared Germany to be a peaceful nation, with no manufacturing or possession of nuclear, biological, or chemical weapons.

This recognition of the Polish border was an important acknowledgement in the eyes of the international community. The frontier between the two countries follows the line of the Oder and Neisse rivers, from the Baltic Sea to Czechoslovakia (present-day Czech Republic). This boundary was drawn when the Allied powers ceded all German lands east of these rivers to Poland after the war. In 1950, the German Democratic Republic (East Germany) unenthusiastically accepted the border. However, West Germany never did.

After the Berlin Wall fell, German chancellor Helmut Kohl was initially reluctant to accept the borders as they had been drawn. He stated that he would only do so under the condition that Poland drop any claims for war reparations. Poland, however, would not budge. Ultimately, people within Kohl's own government, and those in positions of power throughout the world, convinced the chancellor that accepting the border was the best choice to ensure that the newly unified Germany could move forward. Kohl's chief of staff, Chancellery Minister Rudolf Seiters, affirmed, "The border question should be settled in a treaty between an all-German government and the Polish government that puts the seal on the reconciliation of the two peoples. [The Polish people] should know that their right to live in secure borders will not be thrown into question by territorial claims by Germans, either now or in the future."

The United States had formally stated that, without this component of the treaty, it was hesitant to recognize a united Germany. Claiborne Pell, chairperson of the US Senate Foreign Relations Committee, said, "I believe international pressure … contributed to Chancellor Kohl's decision to provide the necessary assurances on the Polish-German border."

When Poland joined the European Union in 2004, the border itself became more of a formality. As of 2016, six hundred seventy thousand Polish nationals were living and working in Germany. Meanwhile, approximately 2.8 million Germans claim Polish roots.

The border between Germany and Poland was a hot-button issue for decades, one that almost undermined Germany's good standing in the international community.

about as a result of the will of the people on both sides of the Iron Curtain:

> Welcoming the fact that the German people, freely exercising their right of self-determination, have expressed their will to bring about the unity of Germany as a state so that they will be able to serve the peace of the world as an equal and sovereign partner in a united Europe; Convinced that the unification of Germany as a state with definitive borders is a significant contribution to peace and stability in Europe …

Other international powers, however, had some reservations prior to the reunification. "We don't want a united Germany," then-British prime minister Margaret Thatcher said. "[S]uch a development would undermine the stability of the whole international situation." French president François Mitterrand's personal adviser shared the sentiment: "France by no means wants German reunification," he said.

The Reunification Process

Regardless, expectations and logistics for creating a united German nation were established, as the complicated process of reunification began. Germans themselves were still adjusting to the idea of becoming a single nation again, in large part because it was unexpected. As late as 1984, a poll conducted in West Germany found that 52 percent of citizens thought

A NEW LIFE

The standards of living were far worse in the east than in the west. East Germany had long been dealing with unusable rivers, pollution, and an increase in cancer and respiratory diseases as a result. However, reuniting as one country meant that those in the east had to adapt to an entirely different political and economic system, which wasn't always easy.

reunification was "unlikely" while 19 percent thought it "impossible."

East Germans, for their part, had to adapt from a command economy—in which a central, public authority controls the means of production—to a market economy, in which private ownership was the norm. They were now permitted to express their opinions freely and become entrepreneurs, but the territory in which they were to be accomplishing these new goals was not fit for the task. Factories and transportation networks in East Germany were in disrepair, and communication networks needed to be updated. The former West Germany would foot the bill for the economic recovery of the eastern territory of this now-united nation. During the 1990s, the German government spent more than 800 billion deutsche marks—then the national currency, equivalent to roughly $801 billion in US dollars today—to upgrade the transportation systems, communication infrastructure, and energy networks, while also funding unemployment payments and providing vocational training for laid-off workers.

A 1991 article in the *US News and World Report* recapped the first six months of reunification from the East German perspective:

> Industrial output has been halved as thousands of companies—from shipbuilders to sweet shops—have proved incapable of surviving against Western competition. And nearly 800,000 eastern Germans are currently unemployed, while an additional 1.8 million people are working shortened hours in a labor force of just under 8 million. By the end of 1991, according to some estimates, more than half of all eastern Germans will be unemployed and only 20 percent of the businesses from the old Communist regime will be operating. To reverse this deterioration, analysts believe that nearly $1.2 trillion will be needed over the next decade to rejuvenate eastern Germany.

The workers from the east seemed unfit to compete with their western counterparts; under the socialist system in which they had lived previously, East Germans had been promised employment and access to social welfare benefits. They weren't used to the competition in a capitalist system. What's more, former West Germans were the ones now being installed in leadership roles in government, business, and education. East Germany had lost an estimated 20 percent of its workforce via emigration from the east to the west, but those seeking economic opportunity often did not find it. Housing options were limited. Kindergartens were full. Despite the fact that the West German population had been declining in recent years, it was not the land of opportunity for all who came looking.

Confronting the Past

Germany also was forced to confront the reputation it had on the international stage. The atrocities committed under the leadership of Adolf Hitler in the name of German superiority and strength had affected millions of lives. Wesleyan University professor William Manchester described other countries' perception of Germany: "There is such thing as national character, but it changes. And the German national character has changed. The Germans are united by language, by culture. And young Germany—which is most of Germany today—is also united by a horror of the Second and Third Reichs."

A history professor from Stanford University, Gordon Craig, noted that repressed German growth had contributed to the horrors of the twentieth century: "The Germans from earliest times were a free and independent people, and dreadful things happened to them, which inhibited those qualities and induced others," Craig wrote. "After the Thirty Years' War, habits of authoritarianism and dependence crept into the behavior of average Germans ... The nation never did have the opportunity to get a political education, as in the English Enlightenment or the American Enlightenment."

Authors, analysts, and historians of the time acknowledged that West Germany had functioned as a proper democracy for a number of years, paving the way for the united Germany to adapt and contribute to the Western world. Another important shift in the country's image on the international stage came in 2000, when Germany revisited its citizenship laws. A change in policy allowed for the children of foreign nationals born in Germany to be granted citizenship, regardless of their ethnicity. In a nation that had long prided itself on its homogenous culture, language, and viewpoint, being a German citizen took on a more modern and progressive meaning.

Meanwhile, Germany moved toward partnering with its neighbors and increasing its prominence in the international community. On November 1, 1993, the terms of the Maastricht Treaty went into effect, forming the European Union. Germany, France, Italy, Belgium, Luxembourg, the Netherlands, Denmark, Ireland, the United Kingdom, Greece, Spain, and Portugal were all members of the EU—and they would soon be joined by others. The goal was to develop a partnership that oversaw economics, politics, diplomacy, defense, justice, and immigration policy. Meanwhile, Germany increased its role in NATO by funding military operations during the Persian Gulf War and participating in a peacekeeping mission in Somalia.

More recently, Germany has been instrumental in peacekeeping missions in Afghanistan.

Measuring the Success of Reunification

In 2015, the Berlin Institute for Population and Development published a study: "How Reunification Is Going: How Far a Once-divided Germany Has Grown Together Again." Its findings show that, despite marked progress, there remains a long way to go. The institute's director summarized the findings and added his personal sentiments:

> There is no example of merging two states with such vastly different political systems that has worked so smoothly. But this reunification was, and continues to be, far more difficult to achieve than was thought during the exuberance of the reunification celebrations. Even if the two parts were only separated for 41 years—that's less than two generations—the citizens of east and west were socialized in such a different way that in retrospect the idea that integration would be swift was utopian.

Of citizens polled for this study, half of all Germans stated a belief that there are more differences than commonalities between easterners and westerners.

In a review of the progress, it appears many of the early issues and inequities remain. In terms of wealth, western Germans remain much more affluent than those in the east. Of the 500 richest Germans, 479 live in the west. Of the twenty most prosperous cities, nineteen are in the west. One of the long-term effects of the socialist regime in the east—the fact that property was typically government-owned—has meant that eastern families generally have little to pass down to their children, unlike those in the west. A wage discrepancy also persists, and factories in the west are much bigger than those in the east. Economists predict these differences will continue to hold back those in the east on an economic level and perhaps even worsen the wage gap.

Perhaps because of these financial differences, Easterners spend 79 percent less on consumer goods than their western neighbors. There are also cultural differences when it comes to what people buy: western Germans spend more money on watches and jewelry, while those in eastern Germany spend more on their gardens.

In some areas, easterners have seen advancement and improvement. The life expectancy of women in the east now matches that of women in the west. Eastern men, however, still have a slightly lower life expectancy than men in the west. Education levels in the east far exceed those of their western counterparts, and easterners have excelled in math, the natural sciences, biology, chemistry, and physics.

Despite different preferences and lifestyles, people throughout the country can say they are German. In commemoration of this fact, Germany celebrates Tag der Deutschen Einheit—Unity Day—every year on October 3, the anniversary of when the unification

Groups in traditional dress celebrate Unity Day on October 3, 2012, in Munich in remembrance of the signing of the unification treaty.

treaty was signed. Unity Day is the only national holiday in Germany; all other holidays are administered by the individual states.

German celebration of this holiday is unlike, for example, Independence Day in the United States. There are no fireworks or military parades, though there are certainly festivals and picnics throughout the country. Germans on both sides of the country are still reconciling what it means to be part of a united nation, but in the era since the Cold War ended and the Berlin Wall fell, Germany has regained its footing in the international community, and in many ways, the people have come to accept one another and their differences.

However, recent elections in 2017 show instability still exists. A political party known as the Alternative

Germany again seems to be experiencing turmoil, as the Alternative for Germany, or AfD, has vocalized its dissent against an open-door policy allowing immigrants and refugees entrance.

for Germany, or AfD, has risen in power in response to German chancellor Angela Merkel's open-door policy for non-Germans seeking asylum. The AfD wants to close off European borders, impose rigorous identity checks along German borders, and set up holding camps abroad to prevent migrants or refugees from attempting to enter Germany. The AfD now holds 13 percent of the seats in the parliament. For those who experienced life in a divided Germany, this idea of exclusion feels like the old way of thinking.

Germany may be at a crossroads once again, though without a wall to divide it this time. Even so, whatever path the country chooses for its political, economic, and social future, it seems it will do so as a single, united nation.

•1815 CE	The German Confederation, comprising thirty-nine city-states, is founded by the Congress of Vienna.
•1849	The Frankfurt Parliament develops Germany's first national constitution.
•1919	The Treaty of Versailles brings an end to World War I. It determines that the Germans must hand over Alsace and Lorraine to France, a pair of Prussian provinces to Poland, and three cities to Belgium. It also requires that Germany pay reparations for its role in the war.
•1933	Adolf Hitler is named German chancellor.
•1939	Under the leadership of Adolf Hitler, Germany invades Poland, effectively starting World War II.
•1945	At the Potsdam Conference June 17–August 2, it is determined that the Allied victors (the United States, Great Britain, France, and the Soviet Union) will divide up postwar Germany and Berlin into four occupation zones.
•1948	The Soviet Union cuts off all land and water access to Berlin on June 24. This will lead to the Berlin airlift, when the Allies are forced to use airplanes to supply West Berlin with food, coal, and other necessities.

•1949   The three Allied zones of postwar Germany officially become the Federal Republic of Germany. The Soviet occupation zone of postwar Germany becomes the German Democratic Republic.

•1953   A workers' revolt takes place across East Germany on June 17. Participants demand better working and living conditions. Their efforts are crushed by GDR leadership with the help of the Soviet Union.

•1961   The border between East and West Berlin is closed on August 13 by barbed wire and fencing. Two days later, the wall is solidified with concrete.

•1961   In a now-famous photograph, East German soldier Conrad Schumann is shown on August 15 leaping over a barbed wire section of the wall into West Berlin. Over the years of the wall's existence, about ten thousand people tried to escape from east to west.

•1963   United States president John F. Kennedy makes a speech on June 26 in West Berlin, stating that citizens should be allowed to travel to the other side of the Berlin Wall. In a display of solidarity, Kennedy says, "All free men, wherever they live, are citizens of Berlin, and, therefore, as a free man, I take pride in the words, 'Ich bin ein Berliner' [I am a Berliner]."

•1963	As of December 17, some visitation is allowed for West Berliners seeking to visit relatives in East Berlin.
•1971	The Four Power accord on Berlin is signed, easing travel restrictions and improving communication between East and West Berlin.
•1985	Mikhail Gorbachev becomes the leader of the Soviet Union.
•1987	United States president Ronald Reagan, speaking in West Berlin on June 12, says: "General Secretary Gorbachev, if you seek peace, if you seek prosperity for the Soviet Union and Eastern Europe, if you seek liberalization: Come here to this gate. Mr. Gorbachev, open this gate. Mr. Gorbachev, tear down this wall."
•1989	Hungary backs out of the Warsaw Pact on September 10, opening the border to Austria for East Germans. Approximately thirteen thousand East Germans flee their country through this route.
•1989	Half a million citizens demonstrate for democracy in East Berlin on November 4.

•1989   Responding to the demonstrations, an East
German government spokesman mistakenly
announces, on November 9, that citizens of
the GDR will be able to travel across the border
without restrictions. Crowds of East Berliners
overwhelm the border guards and begin to
tear down the wall.

•1990   The Unification Treaty is signed on October 3,
as the GDR and the FRG unite to form the
united nation of Germany.

alliance An agreement between two or more nations to cooperate for specific purposes.

amends Compensation for a loss, damage, or injury.

annexation The act of adding to something larger, especially a territory.

armistice A temporary suspension of hostilities; a truce.

Aryan A non-Jewish Caucasian.

asylum A secure retreat.

authoritarianism A way of governance that favors complete obedience rather than individual freedom.

blitzkrieg A swift, intense military attack.

chancellor The chief minister of state in certain governments, including Germany.

cultural assimilation The process by which a person adopts the culture and/or language of another group.

denazification To rid of Nazis and Nazi influence.

détente A period of improved relations among countries during a time of political conflict.

exodus The departure of a large number of people.

glasnost The public policy of the Soviet Union to openly discuss economics and politics.

ideologies The beliefs that guide an individual, social movement, institution, or large group.

imperialism The policy of extending the rule of a nation over foreign countries, often by acquiring other colonies.

industrial Related to general business activities.

Lebensraum A concept or philosophy proposing that additional territory is considered essential for national survival, or for the expansion of trade.

Mein Kampf German for "My Struggle," and the title of Adolf Hitler's autobiography and political manifesto.

perestroika The program of economic and political restructuring in the Soviet Union.

reparations In this case, compensation payable by a defeated country to another country to make up for losses suffered as a result of war.

socialism A system of social and political organization that emphasizes government ownership and control of the community as a whole.

solidarity Unity or agreement of action, feeling, or belief, especially among people with a common interest.

status quo The existing state or condition.

utopian Related to impractical or unrealistic ideals of perfection.

Books

Coy, Jason Philip. *A Brief History of Germany*. New York: Facts on File, 2011.

Garton Ash, Timothy. *In Europe's Name: Germany and the Divided Continent*. New York: Random House, 1993.

Hockenos, Paul. *Berlin Calling: A Story of Anarchy, Music, the Wall, and the Birth of the New Berlin*. New York: The New Press, 2017.

Long, Robert Emmet. *The Reunification of Germany*. New York: Wilson, 1992.

McAdams, A. James. *Germany Divided: From the Wall to Reunification*. Princeton, NJ: Princeton University Press, 1994.

Websites

Fall of the Berlin Wall: It Was Thanks to Soviet Leader Mikhail Gorbachev That This Symbol of Division Fell
http://www.independent.co.uk/news/world/world-history/fall-of-the-berlin-wall-it-was-thanks-to-soviet-leader-mikhail-gorbachev-that-this-symbol-of-9829298.html

Read an analysis of the impact that Soviet premier Mikhail Gorbachev had on German reunification.

German Reunification 25 Years On: How Different Are East and West Really

www.theguardian.com/world/2015/oct/02/german-reunification-25-years-on-how-different-are-east-and-west-really

This article explores how life in both sides of Germany has and has not changed since reunification.

Hitler and "Lebensraum" in the East

http://www.bbc.co.uk/history/worldwars/wwtwo/hitler_lebensraum_01.shtml

This piece considers the philosophy that drove Adolf Hitler to his attempts at a European takeover.

Videos

Fall of the Berlin Wall

http://www.history.com/topics/cold-war/berlin-wall/videos/fall-of-the-berlin-wall

Watch footage from when the Berlin Wall fell.

How Did Hitler Rise to Power?

https://ed.ted.com/lessons/how-did-hitler-rise-to-power-alex-gendler-and-anthony-hazard#review

This lecture analyzes how Hitler ascended to power in Germany.

Tour of East and West Berlin in 1966

https://www.youtube.com/watch?v=Hr8Z2pZcWxM

Explore the differences between the two sides of Berlin during the Berlin Wall era.

Berentsen, William H., and Gerald Strauss. "Germany." Encyclopædia Britannica, December 5, 2017. https://www.britannica.com/place/Germany/The-era-of-partition#ref297778.

Connolly, Kate. "German Reunification 25 Years On: How Different Are East and West Really." *Guardian*, October 2, 2015. https://www.theguardian.com/world/2015/oct/02/german-reunification-25-years-on-how-different-are-east-and-west-really.

Cornwell, Rupert. "Fall of the Berlin Wall. It Was Thanks to Soviet Leader Mikhail Gorbachev That This Symbol of Division Fell." *Independent*, October 30, 2014. http://www.independent.co.uk/news/world/world-history/fall-of-the-berlin-wall-it-was-thanks-to-soviet-leader-mikhail-gorbachev-that-this-symbol-of-9829298.html.

Coy, Jason Philip. *A Brief History of Germany*. New York: Facts on File, 2011.

Feffer, John. "The Costs of German Reunification." *Huffington Post*, November 12, 2014. https://www.huffingtonpost.com/john-feffer/the-costs-of-german-reuni_b_6144764.html.

Garton Ash, Timothy. *In Europe's Name: Germany and the Divided Continent*. New York: Random House, 1993.

Hockenos, Paul. *Berlin Calling: A Story of Anarchy, Music, the Wall, and the Birth of the New Berlin*. New York: The New Press, 2017.

Knighton, Andrew. "11 Countries Invaded by Nazi Germany and Why They Were Invaded." War History Online, April 16, 2016. https://www.warhistoryonline.com/world-war-ii/11-countries-invaded-nazi-germany-invaded.html.

Long, Robert Emmet. *The Reunification of Germany*. New York: Wilson, 1992.

BIBLIOGRAPHY

McAdams, A. James. *Germany Divided: From the Wall to Reunification*. Princeton, NJ: Princeton University Press, 1994.

Noakes, Jeremy. "Hitler and 'Lebensraum' in the East," *BBC*, March 30, 2011. http://www.bbc.co.uk/history/worldwars/wwtwo/hitler_lebensraum_01.shtml.

O'Brien, Michael. *John F. Kennedy: A Biography*. New York: Thomas Dunne Books, 2005.

Ottens, Nick. "Niemals Oder-Neisse: The Border Germany Refused to Accept for 45 Years." *Atlantic Sentinel*, August 23, 2017. http://atlanticsentinel.com/2016/12/niemals-oder-neisse-the-border-germany-refused-to-accept-for-45-years.

"Treaty on the Final Settlement with Respect to Germany: September 12, 1990." U.S. Diplomatic Mission to Germany, November 2003. https://usa.usembassy.de/etexts/2plusfour8994e.htm.

Tuohy, William. "Kohl Retreats, Says He Accepts Polish Borders: Europe: Warsaw Cautiously Welcomes the News. West Germany Will Propose a Formal Treaty Thursday." *Los Angeles Times*, March 7, 1990. http://articles.latimes.com/1990-03-07/news/mn-1895_1_west-germany.

INDEX

ABOUT THE AUTHOR

Jackie F. Stanmyre is a social worker and writer. She worked as an award-winning newspaper reporter at the *Star-Ledger* of Newark, New Jersey, before beginning a career in mental health and addictions treatment. As a juvenile book author, she has written for such book series as Dangerous Drugs, Game-Changing Athletes, Primary Sources of the Abolitionist Movement, It's My State!, and Active Citizenship Today. She lives in New Jersey with her husband and two sons.